NO!
I AM NOT
A
TERRORIST!

Revealing the Myths, Mistruths, and
Misconceptions about Muslims

ZOHRA SARWARI

2nd Edition

ISBN 13: 978-1-935948-50-6
ISBN 10: 1-935948-50-4
LCCN: 2018904754

EMAN
publishing

Printed in the United States of America

NO!
I AM NOT
A
TERRORIST!

Revealing the Myths, Mistruths, and
Misconceptions about Muslims

ZOHRA SARWARI

2nd Edition

Dedication

'Our Lord! Accept this from us. You are the All-Hearing, the All-Knowing.'

The Qur'aan: Chapter 2, Verse 127

ABOUT THE AUTHOR

Zohra Sarwari is an international speaker, established author, creative entrepreneur, energetic life coach to women and children, and savvy business coach to those opening or growing businesses. In her work, she puts into practice what she has learned from her own experiences and education. These include coming to the USA as a child refugee, having four children of her own and homeschooling two of them, and continuing with the other two. She has earned a Bachelor's Degree in Psychology and a Master's Degree in Business Management and is currently working on a Master's Degree in Islamic Studies. Her mission is to serve God by teaching others how to live effectively and productively and to benefit their communities with the gifts with which they are blessed.

REVIEWS

"No! I Am Not a Terrorist! is a warm, witty, and wonderful book that will enlighten and help dismiss the stereotypical understanding many people have of Muslims. Zohra Sarwari shares her personal journey as a proud American Muslim and in doing so breaks our stereotypes, melts our fears, nurtures our hopes, and enlightens our minds and hearts. I highly recommend this book."

Peggy McColl
New York Times Best-Selling Author

"This book goes to great lengths to blur the line between the link to terrorism and any religion. It seeks to demonstrate to its reader that there is truly no religion that condones terrorism. It also addresses how Islaam deals with suicide which would NOT support the act of suicide bombing. I have met the Author, Zohra Sarwari, and can confirm she is a peace loving, responsible mother of some amazing children. In this book, she tells the story the way she feels it needs to be told: with Conviction, Passion, and an eye towards the true source of terrorism. This book will help its reader understand an Authentic Muslim's true point of view on this very sensitive subject."

Mike Tate
Author of *A Unique Renegade*
Thinking into Results Consultant

"This is a MUST READ! Zohra has done an excellent job of taking on the myths which surround Islaam. We all probably know the myths are wrong but she uses the Qur'aan to show us exactly why these misconceptions are false. This is a very informative book that anyone who wants to understand Islaam should read."

Michael J. Schreck, MD
Physician and Personal Development Coach

"In her book, *No! I Am Not a Terrorist!,* Zohra has taken a very brave and paramount step in educating people on the Muslin faith. I applaud her efforts to open people's minds to appreciate the good in all of us."

Paula Weisflock
Author of *Transforming Venus: How to Get Unstuck and Let Your Inner Goddess out to Play*

"A very informative book about the topic of terrorism. Are we being fair when we assume all terrorist acts are perpetrated by Muslims? Obviously, Muslims (25% of the world population) are not all terrorists. Providing you with a historic perspective and using citations from the Koran, Ms. Sarwari answers many questions the reader might have about the Islamic religion: For example, what are its practicing members view of God? What is their level of tolerance towards other religions? How about the status of women? The reader is also confronted with the reality of what it means to be an orthodox Muslim in today's world and asked how they would cope if that was their reality. A MUST READ!"
Louise Belley, Educator

TERMINOLOGY

1. **"ALLAAH"** is the Arabic name for THE ONE SUPREME UNIVERSAL GOD.

2. **"Subhaanahu wa ta'aalaa,"** that mean "He is exalted above weakness and indignity."

3. **Al-Quraan:** The Book of Allaah. A divine guidance for mankind. The Final Testament.

4. **Muslim** is one who has submitted to the Will of **Allaah.**

5. **Allaahu-Akbar** means Allaah is Greater.

6. **Assalaamu 'alaykum** means "Peace be on you." This is a greeting for Muslims. The response to this greeting is *'Wa 'alaykum assalaam,'* which means "and peace be upon you."

7. **Hajj** is one of the five pillars of Islaam, a duty one must perform during one's life-time if one has the financial resources for it. It must be performed during certain specified dates of Dhul-Hijjah (the twelfth month in the Islamic calendar).

8. **Alhamdulillaah** means "Praise is for God!"

9. **JazaakAllaahu khayran** means "May Allaah reward you with good."

10. **Five Daily Prayers: 1.** *Fajr* (pre-dawn): This prayer starts off the day with the remembrance of

Allaah (Subhaanahu wa ta'aalaa); it is performed before sunrise. **2.** ***Dhuhr*** (noon): After the day's work has begun, one breaks shortly after noon to again remember Allaah (Subhaanahu wa ta'aalaa) and seek His guidance. **3.** ***'Asr*** (afternoon): In the late afternoon, people are usually busy wrapping up the day's work, getting kids home from school, etc. **4.** ***Maghrib*** (sunset): Just after the sun goes down, Muslims remember Allaah (Subhaanahu wa ta'aalaa) again as the day begins to come to a close. **5.** ***'Isha*** (evening): Before retiring for the night, Muslims again take time to remember Allaah's (Subhaanahu wa ta'aalaa) presence, guidance, mercy, and forgiveness.

11. **Adhaan** is the call to prayer.

12. **Du'aa** is supplication in Islaam.

13. **Hijaab** refers to a woman's covering.

14. **RadiyAllaahu 'anhu'** meaning "May Allaah be pleased with him."

15. **Bedouin** is one who was born and raised in the desert or mountain wilderness.

16. **In sha' Allaah** means "God Willing."

17. **Niqab** a veil worn by some Muslim women in public which covers everything except their eyes.

18. **Imam** the person who leads the prayers in the mosque.

19. **Ramadan** is the ninth month of the Muslim year (Lunar Calendar) during which Muslims observe fasting from sunrise to sunset. They stay away from food, drink, smoking, and sexual relations.

20. **Tirmidhi, Muslim, Bukhari, Abu Dawood, and other names in parenthesis** are the sources for where I got the sayings of the Prophet Muhammad (Peace and Blessings Be Upon Him). These are authentic sources and can be verified.

INTRODUCTION

CAN I REALLY DO THIS?

There I was at a big conference, thinking about how I would to help women and children achieve their goals and how my book, *9 Steps To Achieve Your Destiny,* could help so many people, Godwilling. As I was sitting there with my 7-year-old imagining my dreams, a lady next to me started asking me questions about my book and what I was doing there. I stopped my daydreaming and started networking with her. When the two guys sitting in front of us overheard our conversation, they also joined in. Then all of a sudden they said something to me that shocked me. One of the guys said to me, "Why aren't you talking about Islam and terrorism?"

I said, "Because my book is about something else. It's a self-help book to empower people, and I want to coach women and kids."

He said, "But right now America is scared of Muslims and we think that you are ALL terrorists. Don't you think you should address this? I mean, you speak English well, you don't have a thick accent, you were raised in the States, and people will be able to understand you. The guys I see on the news all have thick accents and half the time I don't even know what they are saying. Also, the fact that you're a woman will help people not think that Muslim women aren't allowed to speak."

Boom! I was hit with something I didn't even think about. I thought to myself, *Can I really do this? What if they come after me and threaten my life? What if people who hate Muslims came to my events and abused me?* What if, what if, what if, is all I kept thinking about after lunch.

As my daughter and I ate, I asked her what she thought of the idea, and she said she didn't know. So I called my father and asked him, and he said "I don't like this idea. Just stick with what you were doing. You know the FBI, CIA, KGB, MI6 will all be after you. They always follow and hurt those who teach the truth. It's as if they want people to be afraid of Muslims. If you want to do the opposite, then they will find a way to shut you down. I fear for your life. You have three little kids and it's not fair for them to grow up without a mother."

That conversation didn't make me feel much better. It made me really think, should I do this or not? *I mean, I am a practicing Muslim woman. As a matter of fact, many people call me an orthodox Muslim. Also, I have been studying the faith, it's not as I have no knowledge on this subject. However, if I take this route of becoming a professional speaker in this field, that means I must learn more about my faith. I must commit to studying it and earn a degree so I am an expert in the area and not just giving false information.* Lunch break was over and my mind was everywhere. We went back into the conference to learn, but my mind kept wandering off as I looked around the room, *I wonder how many of these people right now think I am a terrorist?* And that was it. I made my decision: I would do this. I would speak about this topic, even though I was putting myself and my family at risk. Why should I fear anyone? It is only God that I should fear as a Muslim. If my Creator is on my side, then no one can harm me, and if He chooses for harm to come my way, then there is also wisdom behind all that He does. I would not allow fear to run my life. I wanted to be a strong Muslim woman who was brave, courageous, and made a difference. I wanted people to know that Muslims are not terrorists, as a matter of fact, we are the opposite if we follow the religion as it was taught to us by the Prophet Muhammad (Peace Be Upon Him). So my journey began...

TABLE OF CONTENTS

CHAPTER 1

Terrorism: What Does It Mean?

It was a Sunday afternoon, and extremely hot outside. Jamila (14 years old) was sitting in her living room, thinking about how she would go to high school this week. It had been a month since 9/11 had happened and everyone was still angry at the Muslims.

"Is it getting too dangerous for me to wear the hijaab (headscarf)? There have been so many hate crimes happening. Women are getting called names, hijaabs are being ripped off the heads, and people are beating up innocent people just because they are Muslim or look Muslim. It's so hard, Mom," she told her mom.

"My dearest, Jamila, how much trust do you have in Allaah, to ask me that question? Remember the hadeeth that was narrated by Abu al-'Abbaas 'Abdullaah bin 'Abbaas (May Allaah be pleased with him): *One day I was riding (a horse/camel) behind the Prophet, peace and blessings be upon him, when he said, 'Young man, I will teach you some words. Be mindful of God, and He will take care of you. Be mindful of Him, and you shall find Him at your side. If you ask, ask of God. If you need help,*

seek it from God. Know that if the whole world were to
gather together in order to help you; they would not be
able to help you except if God had written so. And if the
whole world were to gather together in order to harm you;
they would not harm you except if God had written so.
The pens have been lifted, and the pages are dry.'

(Reported by Tirmidhi)

Jamila, when we are faced with tests we have to remember the teachings of Islaam in order to get our strength," said her mother.

Jamila smiled as she listened to that saying again. She remembered how it made her feel the first time she had heard, "Fear no one but God, and know that should you be in the right, He will always be with you." She kept thinking the killers could not have been Muslims, because Islaam was against this type of oppression and killing. Who was behind this?

Her mother interrupted her thoughts by saying, "It's hard to believe that Muslims could do this. However, there is evil in every culture, faith, gender and society. This will truly be a big test for the Muslims; it will either make our eemaan stronger or weaker. May Allaah make our eemaan stronger, and help us to hold tight to the rope of Allaah. Aameen."

"Alhamdulillaah, Mother, that I have you to remind me. Sometimes it's tough when people stare at me and point at me; they laugh at me and call me names…and I just want to hide at home," Jamila explained herself.

Just being a teenager at high school was tough, but being a Muslim teenager, Jamila was wishing she could be homeschooled or move to another country. Her mind wandered often, thinking, how could others blame her or other Muslims for the crimes other people committed? It doesn't make sense, she would tell herself. Jamila was a senior and she was so excited to get through this last year. However, her normal spirit wasn't there since 911. Her friends distanced themselves from her. Others in school called her a rag head or terrorist. Only two of her friends remained with her, Jennifer and Shelia. Shelia was Muslim too, but she didn't wear the hijaab. So she wasn't bothered as much. When the suggestion came to Jamila to take her own off, she just smiled and said that her hijaab was her strength, a symbol of her faith, her connection to her Lord; without it she would not feel complete. Yet inside she still had fear of what could happen to her.

Each day she would wake up reciting the Qur'aan and praying for strength to get through the day. She would pray and ask Allaah to teach people the truth about Islaam so that they would not hate Muslims and try to hurt them.

....

The Prophet Muhammad (Peace and Blessings Be Upon Him) said:

"He who is deprived of gentleness is deprived of good."

(Muslim)

"Allaah will not show mercy to him who does not show mercy to others."

(Bukhari, Muslim)

"You have two characters which Allaah likes; gentleness and deliberation."

(Muslim)

Gentleness...mercy...deliberation — these are not usually the words most people associate with Islaam and Muslims. Instead, the West is likely to think of words such as *violence, extremism,* and *threat.*

Of course, the media has played a major role in affecting this view. Law-abiding Muslims rarely make the news. Instead, we only see footage the media wants us to see. Why is that? Why do they want people to only see certain views of Muslims? Is it because too many non-Muslim audiences will only read, watch, and click on links to content that shows this particular bigoted viewpoint?

What Does Terrorism Mean?

Terrorism is to instill terror, speaking in a broad sense; it is the use or threatened use of <u>violence</u> in order to attain a political, religious, or ideological aim.

Terrorism is considered a major threat to society, and that's why it is illegal under <u>anti-terrorism laws</u>. Similarly, under "Laws of war" it is considered a <u>war crime</u> when used to target innocent people like <u>civilians</u>, <u>neutral</u> <u>military</u> <u>personnel</u>, or enemy <u>prisoners of war</u>.

There is no universal definition for terrorism.

Different legal systems and government agencies use different definitions. Governments have remained cautious in formulating an agreed upon and legally binding definition. These difficulties arise because the term is politically and emotionally charged.

A **terrorist** is a person who practices "terrorism." "Terrorists" can be from any background, ideology, ethnicity or religion. In the past, many groups have been labeled as terrorists: Irish groups, Russian groups, German groups, American groups, Indian groups, Hispanic groups, Arab groups, Jewish groups, and the list goes on.

In his book, *Inside Terrorism*, Bruce Hoffman defines terrorism in the first chapter: "Mostly the term 'terrorism' is used in terms of being judgmental towards those whom with we disagree or with one's enemies and opponents intentionally in a negative manner."

"What is called terrorism," Brian Jenkins has written, "thus seems to depend on one's point of view. Use of the term implies a moral judgement; and if one party can successfully attach the label terrorist to its opponent, then it has indirectly persuaded others to adopt its moral viewpoint." Therefore, labeling someone or some organization "terrorist" becomes almost unavoidably subjective; it depends on whether one sympathizes with or opposes the person/group/cause concerned. If the victim of the violence gets the sympathy, the act is terrorism. But if the perpetrator of the violent gets the sympathy, then the act is regarded in a more sympathetic, if not positive manner and it is not considered terrorism.

The following aphorism summarizes the judgmental misuse of the word: "One man's terrorist is another man's freedom fighter." An example of such a scenario is when a group using unethical military methods is an ally of a state against a mutual enemy, but when they no longer remain their ally and use those same methods against their former ally, these methods are termed = "terrorism." During World War II, the Malayan People's Anti-Japanese Army was allied with the British, but during the Malayan Emergency, members of its successor, The Malayan Races Liberation Army, were labeled "terrorists" by the British. Similarly, Ronald Reagan and others in the American administration frequently called the Afghan Mujahideen "freedom fighters" during their war against the Soviet Union.

Michael Stohl, Professor of Political Science at UC Santa Barbara, mentions examples of the misuse of the term "terrorism" that include Germany's bombing of London and the U.S. atomic destruction of Hiroshima during World War II.

"Genocide is taking place in Gaza . . . an average of eight Palestinians die daily in the Israeli attacks on the Strip. Most of them are children. Hundreds are maimed, wounded and paralyzed," wrote the Israeli scholar Ilan Pappe.

Next, I would like to go over a few famous terrorist attacks unrelated to Islaam or Muslims.

- We have the Timothy McVeigh case; he bombed the Alfred P. Murrah Federal Building in Oklahoma

City, killing 168 innocent people and injuring hundreds more.

- We have the anti-Sikh riots in Delhi that took place after the assassination of Prime Minister, Indira Gandhi in 1984, when the government took revenge on the minority by allowing Hindu fanatics to slaughter over 55,000 Sikhs and of course rob and destroy their property.

- On April 20, 1999, two students, Eric Harris and Dylan Klebold, killed 12 students and a teacher as well as wounding 23 others before they committed suicide themselves. This was one of the biggest school massacres in the US.

- Jose Flores hijacked Aeromexico Flight 576 after he said a divine revelation came to him. Mr. Flores said he did it because of the date – 9-9-09 – which to him meant the satanic number 666 turned upside down.

- On February 6, 2004, a bomb ripped through a metro train car during the morning commute in Moscow, killing 40 and injuring 112. The bomber, who apparently died in the attack, was believed to be trying to disrupt the upcoming elections in March.

- In San Mateo, a teen armed with a sword and chainsaw in addition to eight pipe bombs strapped to his body was arrested after two explosions went off at San Mateo's Hillsdale High School. More than 1200 students and teachers had to evacuate the school.

A terrorist is one who kills innocent human beings, regardless of age, gender, religion or ethnicity. There is terrorism happening all around us, in our communities, cities, states, and countries.

As you can see, terrorism comes in many forms. However, it always results in the loss of innocent life. No matter where it occurs or what form it takes, terrorism is motivated by complex geo-political considerations that extend far beyond someone's race, creed or nationality.

Rather than lump entire groups into broad categories – as has often happened to Muslim people – we need to recognize that stereotypes are not only unfair, but they are also counterproductive. If we hope to create communities grounded in peace and respect, we cannot judge entire religions or nationalities on the basis of only a few individuals. So I invite you today to begin on a journey of understanding and compassion. One in which each and every person you encounter is accepted on the basis of their own merits instead of preconceived ideas of who and what they are. Join me now as we take the first step to seek common ground.

- There has been a rise in attacks on Muslims. "In London, a van plowed into worshippers near a mosque in the early hours of morning, injuring 11 people, two of them seriously, in what Prime Minister Theresa May said was a "sickening" terrorist attack on Muslims.

  The vehicle swerved into a group of mainly North and West African people shortly after midnight as they left prayers at the Muslim Welfare House and the nearby Finsbury Park Mosque in north London, one of the biggest in Britain.

  The driver, a 47-year-old white man, was grabbed at the scene by locals and pinned down until police arrived." (https://uk.reuters.com/article/uk-britain-security/van-rams-muslim-worshippers-in-londonpm-may-condemns-sickening-attack-idUKKBN19A014)

- There has been a rise in attacks against Muslim women in particular, such as the horrendous attack on Nabra Hassanen, 17, in Virginia, USA.

Nabra was abducted by a man as she and her friends were walking to a suburban Virginia mosque for Ramadan prayers, police said. The man allegedly got out of the car and assaulted the 17-year-old girl as her friends ran to the mosque, where they called police, Wright said.

Her body was found later that afternoon. She had been brutally beaten with a baseball bat, abducted and then beaten with a bat again, this time to death.

As Fairfax County Police and the Loudon County Sheriff's Office searched the area early Sunday, police stopped a man who was "driving suspiciously," Wright said.

Darwin Martinez Torres, 22, was taken into custody as a suspect in the case and subsequently charged with murder, Wright said.

Nabra's father stated, "This is a hate crime." "It's racism, getting killed because she is Muslim."

- Several more hate crimes carried out on Muslim women followed and were reported to police:

Fatima Dhera, 50, a woman tore off her niqab (face veil) while she was shopping at Whole Foods last year, shouting "You cannot do that in this country,"

- Student Aisha Sheikh, 29, said she has seen people driving by unroll their windows and shout, "Go back to your country," and "You don't belong here."

- Maryam Jarady, 39, a businesswoman, said the incidents became more frequent during last fall's presidential election, which Donald Trump won in part by pledging to bar Muslims from entering the country. "People were scared even to go to work," Ms. Jarady recalled.

- Rizwan Jaka, chair of the ADAMS Centre's board, said his 19- and 9-year-old daughters – fourth-generation Americans – have been called "terrorists" and told to "go back to their country." But he said this does not reflect the broader community. (The Globe and Mail)

ACTION PLAN

1. Go to a Mosque or Muslim Student Association and meet a Muslim.

2. Add Muslim pages to your Facebook page and read what they teach, so that you can ask questions.

3. Help report any hate crimes that you witness.

Reflections on this chapter

_____

_____

_____

_____

_____

_____

_____

_____

_____

_____

_____

_____

_____

CHAPTER 2

What About Suicide Bombings?

I was walking in the mall; it was 7 p.m. in the evening. I was holding my three-year-old daughter's hand, and we were looking for a dress for her. As I was walking by the food court, this man stared at me and yelled out, "Do you have a bomb under your dress?"

I just looked at him as tears formed in my eyes. *What a cruel thing to say to me!*

My daughter asked me, "Mommy, what did the man ask you?"

I told her, "Nothing."

How could I explain this to my three-year-old? She would never understand why someone would ask such a question of a random person at the mall. I thought to myself, *Can this really be happening? Do people really think that all Muslims are terrorists? Will it get worse than this?* My mood for shopping was gone, and I just wanted to go home and cry. What if the man had attacked me? What could I have done? How could I have protected myself and my daughter?

As I was driving home, I turned on the Qur'aan on my phone. I was reflecting on the meaning of the verses as the reciter recited them. Tears flowed down my face. Allaah was testing my faith, and I understood. I vowed in the car that day that it was time to take self-defense classes, because there were crazy people out there who could attack me.

"Assalaamu 'alaykum wa rahmatUllaahi wa barakaatuhu," she said as she entered her home with her right foot.

"Wa 'alaykum assalaam wa rahmatUllaahi wa barakaatuhu, honey," replied her husband, Muhammad. "Did you find a dress for Hafsa?" he asked.

Ayesha began crying as she didn't get to buy the dress for her daughter. She became too emotional after her ordeal with the guy asking her if she had a bomb under her dress. Muhammad went over and hugged her, and asked what was wrong. Ayesha told him everything, and Muhammad told her it was time to carry pepper spray with her and took a self-defense class.

"I will go online now and search for some classes in our area. I will also call some of the sisters at the mosque and inform them of the incident that took place so they too can take precautions against something like this or worse happening to them," she said.

"That's a great idea. I will call the Imaam at the masjid and let him know what happened, so that he may let the community know and guide us on how to deal with these types of situations," said Muhammad.

Ayesha realized that this was a big test from Allaah, and that she would have to do more to protect herself and her family. For the first time in her life, she feared for her life and wondered if she would be safe where she lived.

"Yaa Allaah, may you help us. Yaa Allaah, may you give us strength to be able to hold tight to our faith."

Truly, this is a test and we must be patient, she kept saying to herself.

....

"He who commits suicide by hanging himself shall keep on hanging himself in the hellfire (forever), and he who commits suicide by stabbing himself, he shall keep stabbing himself in the hellfire (forever)."

(Bukhari)

Is "suicide bombing: acceptable? I am asked this question so often; I will give you an example of how I answer it. I was sitting with my daughter on a plane and an elderly man in his late sixties was sitting next to me. We began talking about work and life.

A few minutes into the conversation he said, "Honey, let me ask you a question."

I said, "Sure, I'm an open book, ask away."

He thought to choose his words carefully. "How come your people go strapping bombs on themselves and then blow up innocent people with them?"

I smiled and said, "I love this question, and I will answer it in a minute, but I want to ask you something real quick. Is that okay?"

He said, "Sure."

I asked, "How come your people go into the schools killing innocent students, into the mall, drive-by shootings, into other countries killing innocent civilians? How come?"

He looked at me with amazement, as he had no answer. He said, "Well, I never thought about it that way."

I said, "I will answer your question now. First of all, Islaam condemns suicide. Muslims know that during times of sadness, depression or even oppression we need to be patient and let Allaah (*Subhaanahu wa ta'aalaa*) handle the situation. We know that The Almighty is aware of all that is happening, and that He is testing us. With that said, I want you to think a moment about why people commit suicide regardless of who they are.

"Most people do it because they think their life is so hard, that they can't take it anymore. Those who kill innocent people perhaps feel that they have been wronged, and that they have been oppressed, and they want to avenge their oppression. Does that make it right? No, it doesn't! But what you don't hear about in the media is the other side of the story. You hear that a man went into some place and killed himself, but you don't hear about why he did it.

They have witnessed innocent people die all around, them including family, friends, and neighbors killed by the merciless occupying force. They don't have any weapons to fight back, so all they do is suicide bombing…the only weapon that they feel they have. They have lost hope for a peaceful settlement, and realize no one is coming to help them, so they take matters into their own hands and that's when you get the suicide bombing.

"Does this make it right? No, it doesn't. However, when you're being oppressed, you're under occupation, and you have lost your freedom, do you think that you're even in the right mind? Their mosques have been blown up, their schools have been blown up, their homes have been blown up, all they are doing every day is thinking about when it is their turn. I watched a 6-year-old say one time, 'You could never live under these conditions, but we have to.'

"Now, I want you to imagine that's your life, and that is how you're living. You need a lot of faith to not act like that, but when they're trying to erase your faith away with their actions, you feel helpless at the end. So having an empty life with only hatred and revenge is what turns these people to act this way. Basically, they don't know any better. If they knew the consequences of suicide, these kids would not commit it. Does that make sense?"

He said, "Yes, I never thought of it that way. What are the consequences if they commit suicide?"

I looked at my daughter as she waited for the answer. She was 7 years old then. "Well, Prophet Muhammad (Peace Be Upon Him) said: 'He who commits suicide by hanging himself shall keep on hanging himself in the hellfire (forever), and he who commits suicide by stabbing himself, he shall keep stabbing himself in the hellfire (forever).' Think about it; if you are Muslim and you believe in Allaah – God the Greatest, and this is what is said about suicide, does it make sense to do it? Who would like to be in hellfire committing the same act that killed them the first time? The sad part again is that because of how their lives are they're not even aware of this information. Did I answer your question?"

He said, "Honey, you did more than answer it. I had no idea why it was happening, and you just educated me. I hope that you forgive me for my ignorance."

I said, "I do, and it was my pleasure to educate you."

I will tell you what the Qur'aan says about suicide:

'O you who believe, do not consume each other's property illicitly – only mutually acceptable transactions are permitted. You shall not kill yourselves (or another). GOD is Merciful towards you.'

(The Qur'aan: Chapter 4, Verse 29)

'Anyone who commits these transgressions, maliciously and deliberately, We will condemn him to Hell. This is easy for GOD to do.'

(The Qur'aan: Chapter 4, Verse 30)

These verses of the Qur'aan show us that suicide is condemned by Allaah (Subhaanahu wa ta'aalaa); no matter how difficult the situation is, one is to be patient and let Allaah (Subhaanahu wa ta'aalaa) handle it. There are simply no excuses for suicide. The Qur'aan does not promise Paradise to those who commit it but rather warns of condemnation to Hell.

Committing suicide indicates that one does not have faith in Allaah (Subhaanahu wa ta'aalaa), that one is not happy with what Allaah (Subhaanahu wa ta'aalaa) has decreed for him/her. Allaah (Subhaanahu wa ta'aalaa) commands the believer never to despair or lose hope, and instead work for a brighter future:

"None despairs of GOD's Grace except the disbelieving people."

(The Qur'aan: Chapter 12, Verse 87)

With that being said, now I want to go over the history of suicide bombing, where it came from, and why it takes place.

Japan's Kamikaze pilots and their suicide attacks on American warships in the last year of World War 2, remain one of the most terrorizing memories of this war.

The desperate hope that suicide warfare was the way to avoid defeat led the Japanese Army and Navy to adopt its tactics and weapons. In military terms, the idea was similar in most cases: to use a human to precisely guide a powerful explosive weapon all the way to the target in order to achieve a lethal direct hit, and by doing so convert a simple weapon to a guided "smart bomb." The Japanese used the following suicide weapons and tactics in addition to the most successful Kamikaze aircraft:

- Explosive speed boats – a Japanese adoption of the original Italian explosive speed boat. While the Italian naval commandos used explosive speed boats equipped with special eject seats, the Japanese used them as a suicide weapon. Thousands were produced but most were kept for the expected invasion of Japan. They sank eight American ships. This weapon was used several times after World War 2, both with eject seats and as a suicide weapon.
- Suicide torpedoes – this weapon actually preceded the Kamikaze aircraft. Called "Kaiten", these were enlarged torpedoes, fitted with a tiny cockpit and periscope for a suicide operator, and with additional fuel and oxygen and an enormous 3400lb (1530kg) warhead, and launched from a specially modified

submarine or a ship. Hundreds were produced, but they sank just two American ships.

- Suicide midget submarines – with a very high loss rate in their original non-suicide use, a suicide model was developed, carrying explosives instead of attached torpedoes.
- Suicide divers carrying explosives – apparently saw little action and only damaged one American landing craft.
- Suicide infantrymen carrying anti-tank mines – the Japanese Army's suicide weapon. Their goal and motto was "One man – one tank".
- In response to the American landing in Okinawa, which was expected to be the last step before an invasion of Japan, the desperate Japanese High Command ordered on April 6, 1945, that suicide warfare tactics should be employed by ALL branches and units of the Japanese armed forces. The next day, following this command, the Japanese super-battleship Yamato; the largest battleship ever built and armed with the largest guns ever, was sent to a one-way suicide mission in Okinawa. Its purpose was not just to destroy as many American ships as possible, but to also deliberately run aground in Okinawa so that it would be impossible to sink it, so it will be able to continue to fight until literally destroyed. The plan failed when the mighty Yamato was spotted, and then sank by a massive air attack, before reaching Okinawa.
- Another suicide tactic used in this spirit was of fighter aircraft ramming American heavy bombers instead of firing at them.

Nazi Germany also trained and operated suicide pilots shortly before its defeat. The first German suicide unit, the Leonidas Squadron, was established as a squadron of volunteers within the Luftwaffe's top secret special missions air wing (KG200). Its weapon was a manned version of the German jet-powered V-1 cruise missile. This unit trained and reached an operational status, but an approval to use it in combat was never given, mostly because of the availability of Germany's other advanced air-to-ground weapons, that made its operation an unnecessary loss of pilots' lives. The German arsenal of advanced air-to-ground weapons included radio-guided bombs, radio-guided missiles, and the Mistel, an unmanned medium bomber with a huge warhead in its nose, that was piloted by a pilot seated in the cockpit of a fighter aircraft mounted over the unmanned bomber. After guiding the bomber to its final dive at the target, the pilot detached the fighter and flew back to base, while the unmanned bomber crashed and exploded on the target. In a sharp contrast with minimally trained suicide pilots, these unmanned bombers were successfully flown by very experienced bomber pilots, who indeed achieved a relatively high success rate, sinking ships and destroying strategic bridges.

The other German suicide unit, which did see combat action, was the Luftwaffe's fighter wing 300 (JG300) that was ordered, shortly before the end of the war, to use ramming tactics against allied heavy bombers. This tactic was used just a few times and its success rate was not high.

The military and cultural rationale of suicide warfare

The **military rationale** of suicide warfare of all types, both historically and now, is simple. When planning attacks against what is considered high value enemy targets, military planners often lack truly adequate military resources required to achieve success. This lack is normally bridged by resourcefulness and military talent, and by a greater sacrifice of soldiers. But in extreme cases, and if the mission is not cancelled due to extreme lack of resources, extreme measures are required, measures which would not be used if better alternatives were available. This is true both for a military planner who plans to attack a military target, and for a terrorist leader who plans to mass murder civilians. As long as they had relatively significant military forces, even if inadequate, the Japanese did not turn to suicide warfare. Sacrifice yes, but not suicide. They switched to the Kamikaze suicide tactics only when their disadvantage became so severe that even common sacrifice of soldiers was simply not enough, and a radical new weapon (guided missiles) was essential, and in its absence, they used the Kamikaze pilots as a substitute...The other key element of suicide warfare is the **cultural rationale**. Suicide warfare is used only by human societies which face an immediate threat that is **perceived** by them as being so severe that they believe they are facing **extinction**, whether cultural or physical, or a similar mass destruction.

They used suicide bombing, because they were significantly weaker than their enemies, technologically, economically, and therefore eventually militarily, or otherwise they would not have to fight like that. (http://www.2worldwar2.com/kamikaze-pilots.htm)

With that being said, the number of Muslims who carry out suicide bombing are relatively small compared to the Japanese Kamakazi pilots, the Vietcong Tamil Tigers, and other groups. The Tamil Tigers "have the distinction of introducing suicide bombing as a tactic, and have carried out more suicide bombings than Hamas, Islamic Jihad, and al-Qaeda combined." (http://en.wikipedia.org/wiki/Liberation_Tigers_of_Tamil_Eelam)

The next time you hear of a suicide bombing, please don't think it's a Muslim thing; rather, it is a military war tactic that many fighting groups use. What one needs to remember is that it is against Islaam to commit suicide; in Islaam it is prohibited and there is a severe punishment for it.

ACTION PLAN

1. Continue to educate yourself around what Islaam is.

2. Study different cultures and religions that may have similar practices.

Reflections on this chapter

_____

_____

_____

_____

_____

_____

_____

_____

_____

_____

_____

_____

_____

CHAPTER 3

Jihad – Now What Does That Mean?

Finally, a quiet day with no kids! is what I was thinking. *I can write my book, and have peace and quiet for a few hours.* I smiled at the thought. It had been a while since I had some time alone. Well, what I didn't say was *In'sha'Allaah (God Willing).*

As I was in middle of writing several sentences, I heard shouts and a boy pleading for someone to stop. As much as I wanted to just close my window and block out all of the noise and focus on writing my book, I knew I had to see what was going on.

So I walked over and looked out the window. To be honest with you, I sort of rushed and forgot to wear my hijab. At that moment, I thought I would just glance out the window and then go back to work. However, what I saw next was shocking to me. When I heard the boy at first, I thought maybe some kids took his toy and he was pleading for it.

To my surprise, there seemed to be about six or seven boys against one. These boys were all between the ages of eleven and thirteen. Two of them were holding him down while the rest were calling him names and hitting him. As I saw this, I was so upset that I yelled out, "Hey, what are you guys doing? Are you seriously all ganged up against one boy, all of you?"

They stopped what they were doing and looked around. They were trying to find out who was talking to them.

I yelled out, "I am up here! It is 10 am Saturday morning and instead of going to the library to get books or playing together, you're fighting? Isn't it time to do something good with your lives? I am sure that your parents don't know that you're doing this right now."

At this time, the boy who had been being beaten up slowly ran away, a s they had released him. He was listening as well, but he knew if he didn't escape it might be harder to later.

The boys continued to listen to me, and then I praised them for listening and said I knew they would do amazing things in life. They needed to spend their time wisely and have goals and dreams for the future.

After what have seemed like hours, the boys departed on their way. They seemed to spread out and think as they left.

"On the authority of Abu Sa'eed al-Khudree (may Allaah be pleased with him) who said: I heard the Messenger of Allaah (peace and blessings of Allaah be upon him) say,

'Whosoever of you sees an evil, let him change it with his hand; and if he is not able to do so, then [let him change it] with his tongue; and if he is not able to do so, then with his heart — and that is the weakest of faith.'"
(Muslim)

This is what the word "Jihad" means to me. We must all help against oppression wherever we can.

………………………………………………………………..

9/11: a day that we as Muslims will never forget, a day that the words "jihad" and "terrorism" came to the forefront of Western understanding. "Jihad" became a word that would ring throughout years to come.

"Jihad" is one of the most misunderstood and misinterpreted words that is used against Muslims spanning the globe and particularly in Western societies.

The most common interpretation that is given is "Holy War," a statement that has been used and reused since the beginning of the Crusades and even before in the reign of the Greeks.

In order to look at the word "jihad," let's first understand what does "holy war" mean?

Well, there are many interpretations for this statement:

Cambridge Dictionary:
A war fought to defend religious beliefs or
to force others to follow a different religion.

Merriam-Webster:
A war or violent campaign waged often by religious extremists for what is considered to be a holy purpose.

Now the Collins dictionary breaks it down into interpretations by region:

- A **holy war** is a war that people fight in order to defend or support their religion.

(in British)
- (Noun) A war waged in the cause of a religion.

(in American)

- A war <u>fought</u> on <u>behalf</u> of a religion or for a religious cause.
- Any <u>zealous</u> or <u>fanatical</u> <u>campaign</u>.

The Random House dictionary:
ho'ly war`
n.
1. A war waged for what is supposed or proclaimed to be a holy purpose, as the defense off a faith.
2. Any disagreement or argument between fanatical proponents of radically differing beliefs, opinions, etc.

Literal Meaning of Jihad

Now when we look at "jihad," we must understand the root of the word. As Arabic is a Semitic language, like Hebrew, they both are derived from a **triliteral** or triconsonantal root and then predefined molds that verbs are constructed with that root. Each root has a general meaning.

Let's look at the root word for jihad. The Arabic word "jihad" is a noun. Its singular past tense verb is "jahada" (masculine) or "jahadat" (feminine). The singular active participle of "jihad" is "mujahid" (masculine) or "mujahida" (feminine). The root of the word "jihad" is "juhd," which means "effort." Another related word is "ijtihad," which means "working hard or diligently."

Jihad is simply the process of "exerting the best efforts," involving some form of "struggle" and "resistance," to achieve a particular goal. In other words, jihad is the struggle against, or resistance to, something for the sake of a goal. The meaning of the word is independent of the nature of the invested efforts or the sought goal.

That is, contrary to common belief, the word "jihad" does not necessarily imply any violent effort, let alone "war" and such instances of extreme violence.

It is a general term that can mean violent as well as peaceful actions, depending on the context in which it is used, as we shall indeed see later. Thus "jihad" as a generic word can be used even when the sought goals are not Islamic, i.e. in non-religious contexts. (this article is from the second edition of *Jihad in the Qur'an: The Truth from the Source*)

When we look at the English interpretation of the word jihad, Holy War, the word has been misused.

The concept of jihad has been taken out of context and used by many political and religious groups over the ages to justify various forms of violence.

In most cases, Islamic splinter groups invoked jihad to fight against the established Islamic order. Scholars say this misuse of jihad contradicts Islam.

When we look at Arabic while following the rules for the Semitic languages, we understand that with this interpretation, the root word in Arabic would be *war*, which is "al-harb".

Now recognizing that the root word for Jihad means effort, struggle or resistance,

we understand that jihad is not a violent concept. "Jihad" is not a declaration of war (harb) against other religions, but in fact the linguistic meaning of the word is more about self-preservation.

When I spoke to Muslim teens about "jihad," many of them stayed away from the word. "Envisioning Muslims acting out of context and causing harm to others in particular the Western nations," one Muslim teen said, "this is our interpretation of the word, and not having any background in Islamic knowledge or understanding." The rest of the group agreed. "Being raised in the West and having little understanding of the true teaching of the religion, we are left with an interpretation, even if incorrect, that is widespread and spoken about again and again by the media."

As I delved into researching this word within the Muslim community, I saw how far-reaching a misinterpretation can go, even within the community that it is being used against.

The misinterpretation and widespread misunderstanding of this term has caused a lot of fear, and through fear, a lot of violence.

The basic understanding and education of those inside and outside of the faith is most important. We must understand that the one who adheres to, understands and practices what Islam upholds also conducts themselves through the values of reason, balance, and responsibility and helps and instructs us to uphold those values for ourselves and the community in our conduct of worldly affairs.

"Permission is granted to those who are fighting because they have been oppressed....those who have been expelled from their homes without any just cause."

(The Qur'aan: Chapter 22, Verses 39-40)

It is explained most eloquently by the beloved Prophet (Peace Be Upon Him) who said,

"The best of jihad is a just word spoken to an unjust ruler."

(Abu Dawood)

And at another time,

"The mother of the faithful believers: The Prophet (Peace and Blessings Be Upon Him) was asked by his wives about

the Jihad and he replied, "The best Jihad (for you) is (the performance of) Hajj."

(Bukhari)

"Indeed, among the greatest types of Jihad is a just statement before a tyrannical ruler."

(Tirmidhi)

Jihad in the Qur'aan

When we look into the Qur'aan, we find many verses of instruction concerning Jihad and the legal meaning or Sharia meaning.

When the non-Muslims of Mecca waged war against the Prophet and his followers in Medinah, these verses gave the Muslims permission to defend themselves. This is after years and years of persecution, torture, and torment.

Again Allaah says,

"Fight in the way of God those who are fighting against you; and do not exceed (the limits). Verily, Allaah does not love those who exceed (the limits)."

(The Qur'aan: Chapter 2, Verse 190)

Again, another verse responding to an act of war, giving Muslims clear guidelines and limitations. When defending ourselves, Allaah warns us not to "exceed" the limits.

In one of the most beautiful ayahs explaining and instructing Muslims even in the mode of defense during war, Allaah says,

"But if they incline to peace, then you incline to it, and put your trust in Allaah."

(The Qur'aan: Chapter 8, Verse 61)

When looking at any religious text, we must make sure we understand the text within its full context. This helps dispel any ignorance and possible fear around a word that has been widely misused and misrepresented in these times.

ACTION PLAN

1. Try to understand the Arabic terminology that is being used by others.

2. Ask about the context it is used in.

<u>Reflections on this chapter</u>

_____

_____

_____

_____

_____

_____

_____

_____

_____

_____

_____

_____

CHAPTER 4

Truths About Myths & Misconceptions!

"9 11, how can I help you?" said the dispatcher.

"There is a fire at our mosque and it's growing quickly. Please send the fire department!" yelled Fatima.

"Ma'am, please calm down. So you're telling me that the mosque is on fire?" said the dispatcher.

"Yes, someone set the mosque on fire," said Fatima.

"What is the address for the mosque?" the dispatcher asked.

"It's 1220 N State College Blvd, Anaheim, CA 92806. Please tell them to hurry," said Fatima.

"Ma'am, I need you to calm down and tell me, is there anyone in the building?" the dispatcher asked.

"No, it's empty," Fatima replied as tears rolled down her face in sorrow at seeing the house of Allaah burning.

"Okay, ma'am, the police and fire department are on their way," said the dispatcher.

"Thank you," Fatima replied as she hung up the phone.

How hard we have worked to make this possible. How hard we have worked to ask for donations and to make this mosque. It has served so many people and has been a home for so many people throughout the years. Tears kept rolling down her face. *How could anyone do this to the house of God? What if someone was inside there? After 9/11, hate crimes have gone up tremendously against the Muslim community. However, we never thought it could happen to us.* Fatima's thoughts were interrupted as she looked over and saw Maryam crying, talking to her husband, Ahmad.

"Ahmad, what if they start the fire next time while we are in the masjid? What if they burn our homes? What if they burn our cars?" Maryam asked her husband in a panicked voice.

"Don't worry, honey, Allaah will protect us. We must trust in Him and know that He will help us in times of difficulty. The person who did this was an ignorant person, and they will catch him, in shaa' Allaah," Ahmad replied.

Ahmad was thinking to himself, *If they only knew what Islaam was really about, they would never have done this. How to reach out to these people, when the media is so negative about Islaam and Muslims? No matter how much we try, we can't get too much of the mainstream media to explain the real Islaam.*

"Ahmad, if we don't teach the real Islaam to these people, we will have more hatred, pain and suffering towards the Muslims. Where do we start?" Maryam asked.

She looked around, seeing each member of the community in fear, and wondered where they would be praying this Ramadan. *God's house has been destroyed, where will we all meet to pray as a community now?*

If only the perpetrator came to the mosque and asked questions about Muslims and Islam, this whole incident could have been avoided. Education truly opens the mind and teaches tolerance to the majority, Maryam kept thinking until the sirens interrupted her. *"Alhamdulillaah,"* she said to Ahmad.

"All praise truly belongs to God alone. He will help us rebuild His home again. We must have faith and work hard. He will make the rest happen, in shaa' Allaah," Ahmad added.

....

There are many misconceptions surrounding Islaam and Muslims; I will be writing about seven of them. Please read them carefully, for many people's views of Islaam and Muslims are distorted, and will hopefully be corrected in the next few pages, *in shaa' Allaah* (God Willing).

The Messenger of Allaah (Peace Be Upon Him) said the following two quotes:

"Righteousness is good character, and sin is that which lingers in your heart and which you do not want people to know."

(Muslim)

"He is not of us who does not show mercy to our little ones and respect to our elders."

(Tirmidhi)

"False history gets made all day, any day, the truth of the news is never on the news."

Adrienne Rich

MISCONCEPTION #1:

Muslims are intolerant of others' faiths.

"There is no compulsion in religion."

(The Qur'aan: Chapter 2, Verse 256)

"And if your Lord had so willed, He could surely have made mankind one Ummah [nation or community (following one religion only, i.e. Islâm)], but they will not cease to disagree."

(The Qur'aan: Chapter 11, Verse 256)

"And had your Lord willed, those on earth would have believed, all of them together."

(The Qur'aan: Chapter 10, Verse 99)

Allaah (Subhaanahu wa ta'aalaa) explains the freedom of choice in choosing one's faith.

The Prophet, Muhammad (Peace Be Upon Him) said,

"Love for humanity what you love for yourself."

(Bukhari)

That means to treat people the way you want to be treated. Islaam is a way of life for Muslims; in everything that we do, we try to do it for the sole purpose of pleasing Allaah (Subhaanahu wa ta'aalaa). We know that Allaah (Subhaanahu wa ta'aalaa) is always watching, and He has told us how to behave through the example of the Prophet Muhammad (Peace Be Upon Him). The Qur'aan tells Muslims that they are not the only ones who worship God; the Jews and Christians also worship Him.

MISCONCEPTION #2:

Islam oppresses women.

The Prophet, Muhammad (Peace Be Upon Him) said,

"The most perfect in faith amongst believers is he who is best in manner and kindest to his wife."

(Tirmidhi)

Most of the stories that you hear about the ill-treatment of women in "Muslim" countries have to do with their local culture and traditions, and has no basis in Islaam. Spousal abuse, forced marriages, and restricted movement directly contradict Islamic Law governing family behavior and personal freedom.

One thing to remember is that these atrocities also exist in other cultures, even in the West. However, in such cases the faith of the perpetrator is rarely mentioned. Instead, these cases are considered isolated acts of abuse committed by individuals. Religion is only relevant when a Muslim commits them.

In Islaam, when a woman gets married, the groom gives her a gift for her personal use. She can basically ask for whatever she wants. The woman also gets to keep her own last name rather than taking her husband's last name; after all, it is her identity that she was raised as. Islaam sees a woman, whether single or married, as an individual in her own right, with the right to own and dispose of her property and earnings.

Both men and women are told to dress in a way that is modest and dignified. Also, women only wear the hijab or niqab when they are outside. Violence towards women and forcing them to do anything against their will is not allowed. According to the rulings of Islaam, a girl must not be forced to get married against her will. Her parents only suggest suitors who they think will be a good fit for their daughter; the final answer is up to the woman!

MISCONCEPTION #3:

The crescent moon is a symbol of Islaam.

The early Muslims had on their flags the writing, ***"There is no God worthy of worship but Allaah."*** This was their identification. The crescent moon and star symbol pre-dates Islaam by several thousand years, and it was not affiliated with Islaam at all until the Ottoman Empire placed it on their flag. So no! It is not a symbol of Islaam.

MISCONCEPTION #4:

All Muslims are Arabs.

There are 1.6 billion Muslims in the world. One out of every four people is a Muslim. About 18% of the Muslim world is actually Arab; 27.4% of the Muslim population is in Africa, 69.1% of Muslims are in Asia, 2.8 % of Muslims are in Europe, and less than 2% are in North America and Latin America.

MISCONCEPTION #5:

Muslims worship a different God.

Allaah is the Arabic word for the proper noun, "The God of the universe." He is the One and Only God worthy of worship, without any partners. He is the God of the entire universe and all of mankind. He, the Exalted, does not get tired, nor does He have a son as the Christians believe, nor does He have any associates. He does not have human-like attributes as found in other faiths.

Lastly, Muslims believe in all the previous Prophets and Messengers (PBUT) sent by Allaah (Subhaanahu wa ta'aalaa) to guide mankind, including, but not limited to Adam, Abraham, Solomon, Lut, Noah, Job, Joseph, Moses, John the Baptist, Jesus (PBUT), and many more, with Prophet Muhammad (PBUH) being the seal of the Prophets.

MISCONCEPTION #6:

Muslims don't believe in Jesus (PBUH).

The Qur'aan talks about Jesus (*Isa* in Arabic) (Peace Be Upon Him), his miraculous birth, his teachings, and the miracles he performed by Allaah's (Subhaanahu wa ta'aalaa) Permission. Jesus (Peace Be Upon Him) was born miraculously through the same "Power" that Adam (Peace Be Upon Him) was created. Ask yourself this question, why isn't Adam (Peace Be Upon Him) God's son? He (Peace be Upon Him) was created without a mother and a father, and he (Peace be Upon Him) was the first human to be created.

The Qur'aan tells us that Jesus (Peace Be Upon Him) said to the children of Israel:

"I have come to you with a sign from your Lord: I make for you out of clay, as it were, the figure of a bird, and breathe into it and it becomes a bird by God's leave. And I heal the blind, and the lepers, and I raise the dead by God's leave."

(The Qur'aan: Chapter 3, Verse 49)

For Muslims, neither Muhammad (Peace Be Upon Him) nor Jesus (Peace Be Upon Him) were sent to change the basic doctrine of belief in One God that was brought by earlier Prophets (Peace be Upon Them); instead they were sent down to confirm and renew it.

There is even a chapter in the Qur'aan named after his mother, Mary (*Maryam* in Arabic).

The Qur'aan describes the "Annunciation" as follows:

"Behold!" the Angel said, "God has chosen you, and purified you, and chosen you above the women of all nations. O Mary, God gives you good news of a Word from Him whose name shall be the Messiah, Jesus, son of Mary, honored in this world and the Hereafter, and one of those brought near to God. He shall speak to the people from his cradle and in maturity, and shall be of the righteous."
She said: "O my Lord! How shall I have a son when no man has touched me?"
He said: "Even so; God creates what He wills. When He decrees a thing, He says to it, "Be!" and it is."

(The Qur'aan: Chapter 3, Verses 42-47)

In the Qur'aan, Allaah (Subhaanahu wa ta'aalaa) has said that Jesus (Peace Be Upon Him) was a Prophet, just like the many other Prophets (Peace Be Upon Them) that were sent to mankind to guide people to the right path and to teach people to worship God, and God alone.

MISCONCEPTION #7:

Muslims don't care about education and making a difference in their societies.

The Messenger of Allaah (Peace Be Upon Him) said:

"Seeking 'ilm (knowledge) is incumbent on every Muslim."

(Ibn Hajar Al-'Asqalani)

> *"Among every **four humans in the world, one of them is Muslim**. Muslims have increased by over **235** percent in the last fifty years up to nearly 1.6 billion. By comparison, Christians have increased by only 47 percent, Hinduism, 117 percent, and Buddhism by 63 percent. Islam is the second largest religious group in France, Great Britain and USA (Muslims in USA are 8 million and Jews are 6 million)."*
>
> http://www.islamicweb.com/begin/results.htm
> (emphasis in the original)

Among the reasons that Islaam has grown so rapidly is the simplicity of its creed, the belief in one God Who is the Only One worthy of worship. Islaam also tells mankind to use their intelligence and continually learn. When Islaam began to grow and its message was spreading, it was then that universities began to flourish and civilizations began to emerge and prosper. I will give you a few examples of what

Muslims have contributed to society: algebra, the Arabic numerals, and also the concept of zero (which was vital to the advancement of mathematics). These were concepts discovered by Muslims and then spread to different European civilizations who utilized them. Other discoveries include the astrolabe, the quadrant, and high quality navigational maps.

"Peace cannot be kept by force. It can only be achieved by understanding."

Albert Einstein

Abdullah ibn Amr reported: The Messenger of Allaah, (Peace And Blessings Be Upon Him) said,

"Whoever would love to be saved from Hellfire and admitted into Paradise, then let him die with faith in Allaah and the Last Day, and let him treat people the way he would love to be treated."

(Muslim)

ACTION PLAN

1. Don't assume things about others because TV, websites on the internet, social media, radio or other media say it.

2. Do your due diligence and research before you judge or take an opinion about anything.

3. Go to the mosque and speak to someone about things you may have heard about.

4. Join a Muslim newsletter to understand what is happening in the Muslim communities within your area.

Reflections on this chapter

_____

_____

_____

_____

_____

_____

_____

_____

_____

_____

_____

CHAPTER 5

The Headscarf (Hijaab)

"Take that rag off your head. This is America, and we don't dress that way!" yelled a man as he boarded the plane.

Khadija turned around to see who was talking to her. As she looked at him, she wondered how to reply. It wasn't even 30 seconds later that he walked up the aisle of the plane to her and just pulled off her hijaab (headscarf).

Khadija was speechless, and as she grabbed for her hijaab, she was crying. The woman next to her felt sorry for her and started yelling at the man.

"Who are you to touch her? To take her headscarf off of her head? This is a free country and she can practice her religion as she chooses to!" she yelled.

By now the flight attendants came and intervened and had the man moved to a seat in the back. They tried to calm Khadija down. She was crying and holding her daughter's hand.

She kept looking back to see if he would come back. *What if he hits me this time? What if he stabs me? What if he hits my daughter? What will I do if I need to go to the bathroom?* These thoughts and more were inside her head. *I won't be able to sleep on the plane; I won't be able to use the restroom, Yaa Allaah.*

"Yaa Allaah, protect me, Yaa Allaah protect me, as I wear the hijaab to please You alone," Khadija called out secretly to Allaah.

Moments later, a male flight attendant accompanying a female flight attendant came to Khadija and asked her if she needed anything: the restroom, drinks, snacks. They really tried to comfort her. She was thankful to Allaah that He sent her people who cared and made her feel at ease.

Truly God is Great, she said silently to herself.

This lady behind her took out a chocolate to give her and her daughter. She thanked her. Another man was walking by and he told her he would escort her out of the airplane to her car so that she didn't need to feel alone.

All of these wonderful people whom Allaah has put love in their hearts for others. She thanked Allaah for them.

"You must not lose faith in humanity. Humanity is an ocean; if a few drops of the ocean are dirty, the ocean does not become dirty."

Mohandas K. Gandhi

Khadija knew this was just a test from Allaah, and that she would have to hold even tighter to her faith. She remembered the hadeeth of the Prophet Muhammad (Peace Be Upon Him):

"There will come a time when holding on to your eemaan (belief) will be like holding on to hot coals."

(Tirmidhi)

That time has come, Khadija thought to herself. *To be a practicing Muslimah or Muslim man, one has to be really careful. On the one hand, you have Satan trying to dismay you from taking this path. Then, on the other hand, you have the people who are ignorant and due to their ignorance are trying to harm the Muslims. All we can do is be patient and do the right thing at all times, and remember that Allaah loves those who are patient. We cannot give up being who we are, and following the example of the Prophet Muhammad (Peace Be Upon Him), because of one bad person.*

....

"Sometimes risk taking may involve the most simple of acts. Yet we often whip up a bag full of excuses to avoid taking action. For goodness sake (literally), let's step beyond our security bubbles and start reaching out to those who cross our path."

Chelle Thompson, Editor of *Inspiration Line*

Often I get the stares, the looks, as I am walking. I could be at the mall in Indiana, or at the airport. I could be eating in a restaurant, or playing with my kids at Chuck E. Cheese's. The point is, people just find it strange, and they look at it that way.

Amazingly, one day I took my daughter and sister-in-law with me to go and volunteer at a nursing home.

A lady who resided there walked up to me and said, "Why do you wear that?"

I asked, "Wear what?"

She said, "That thing on your head?"

I replied with yet another question, "Do you believe in God?"

She said, "Yes!"

I said, "Wonderful! What religion do you believe in?"

She replied, "I am Christian."

I said, "Great. So you believe in Jesus Christ (Peace Be Upon Him), correct?"

She said, "Yes, I do."

I said, "Okay, so let me ask you a question, how did his mother, Mary (Peace Be Upon Her) dress? In every picture that I have seen of Mary, she is fully clothed in modest clothing and her head is covered, correct?"

She smiled and said, "Yes, but that was then, and times have changed now, and you don't need to be dressed that way anymore." This whole time, my daughter, sister-in-law, and some of the nurses were watching the entire scene. I was amazed at how this 80+-year-old woman was thinking.

I looked at her and said, "The reason that I wear the headscarf is to obey God. God has told us to wear it. One of the reasons He tells us to cover ourselves is so that we are not harassed… It is for our own modesty and protection."

She stared at me more angrily than before and said, "I still don't agree, I don't think you need to wear it. We are in different times, and it is not necessary to wear."

I glanced at her and said, "That is your opinion and you're entitled to it, but as for me, I want to obey the commands of God the Greatest. I have to get going now, you have a great day."

My daughter looked at me and said, "Momma, why was she so mean? Why did she tell you to take it off? She said she believed in God, doesn't she know we want to please God?"

I said, "Honey, people are entitled to their opinion, we need to respect them for who they are, and we want them to respect us for who we are. If she cannot understand why we do it, then there is nothing else we can do besides clarifying our point of view. If they still insist on their opinion, we must agree to disagree."

Alya smiled and said, "Okay, Mom."

*"Judge me by what is **IN** my head, not what is **ON** my head."*

(Unknown)

Muslim Woman's Clothing Requirements

Clothing:

The whole body should be covered, except for the face and hands. Some scholars also believe that the hands and face should be covered as well. Garments should not be transparent in anyway. Clothing should not be tight-fitting.

It is also important that the following aspects of dress be considered as well: Any veil which in itself may become an attraction is to be avoided. Clothing should not be perfumed when one is outdoors or around men who are not immediate family. Deodorant can be used. The form of dress should not in any way resemble that of men.

Allaah (Subhaanahu wa ta'aalaa) says in the Qur'aan in Chapter 33, Verse 59:

"Oh Prophet, tell your wives and your daughters and the women of the believers to draw their outer garments close around them. That will be better, that they may be known

*(as chaste, believing women) and not be abused. And
Allaah is Oft-Forgiving, Most Merciful."
"And tell the believing women to lower their gaze (from
looking at forbidden things) and protect their private parts
(from illegal sexual acts, etc.) and not to show off their
adornment except what must (ordinarily) appear thereof,
that they should draw their veils over their bosoms."*

(The Qur'aan: Chapter 24, Verse 31)

Asma, daughter of Abu Bakr (may Allah be pleased with
them both) came to see the Messenger of Allaah (Peace Be
Upon Him). She was wearing a thin dress; the Prophet
(Peace Be Upon Him) turned away from her and said:

*"O Asma, once a woman reaches the age of puberty no
part of her body should be uncovered except her face and
hands."*

(Abu Dawood)

Virtues of wearing the *hijaab:*

1. As an act of submission to Allaah (Subhaanahu wa
    ta'aalaa) – God the Greatest.

2. Allaah (Subhaanahu wa   ta'aalaa) says in the
    Qur'aan:

*"And tell the believing women to lower their gaze (from
looking at forbidden things) and protect their private parts
(from illegal sexual acts, etc.) and not to show off their*

*adornment except what must (ordinarily) appear thereof,
that they should draw their veils over their bosoms."*

(The Qur'aan: Chapter 24, Verse 31)

3. An act of obedience to the Prophet Muhammad
    (Peace Be Upon Him), because he relayed the
    message from Allaah (Subhaanahu wa ta'aalaa) to
    us.

4. Allaah (Subhaanahu wa ta'aalaa) made adherence to
    the *hijaab* a manifestation of chastity, modesty and
    protection against being molested or harassed. As
    Allaah (Subhaanahu wa ta'aalaa) says:

*"O Prophet! Tell your wives and your daughters and the
women of the believers to draw their cloaks (veils) over
their bodies (when outdoors). That is most convenient that
they should be known and not molested."*

(The Qur'aan: Chapter 33, Verse 59)

Allaah (Subhaanahu wa ta'aalaa) says in the Qur'aan:

*"Be not soft in speech, lest he in whose heart is a disease
(of hypocrisy or evil desire) should be moved with desire,
but speak in an honorable manner."*

(The Qur'aan: Chapter 33, Verse 32)

From the above verse, we see that the *hijaab* is a
mode of protection for women and has been ordered
to protect women from being molested and being

perceived as sex objects. Also, a woman only wears the hijab or niqab when there are other men whom she can possibly have relations with. So at home, at an all-girls party, or with immediate family (ex, brother, father, grandfather, nephews or uncles) she doesn't wear the hijab.

5. The *hijaab* makes for greater purity of heart for the believing men and women because it screens against the low desires of the heart.

Now you know a few of the reasons why Muslim women wear the *hijaab*; the more they cover the more they feel they are pleasing Allaah (Subhaanahu wa ta'aalaa) – God the Greatest. Here are some struggles that Muslim girls and women face in today's society.

Struggles of Muslim Women in Today's Society:

1. In Singapore, on Feb 1 2002, several 7-year-old Muslim girls were kicked out of school for wearing the hijaab. The deputy prime minister had banned it. Amazingly, while he did this to the Muslim girls, at the same time he allowed the Sikh boys to continue wearing their turbans.

   Many Muslim parents are now forced to send their daughters to Malaysia just so they can have the freedom to practice their religion and learn at the same time. Is that fair?

2. Feb 2002; in Spain, a 13-year-old Muslim girl was not allowed to enter school wearing the hijaab. The school and the education minister condemned the hijaab as "a sign of discrimination against women" and declared that to allow the girl to wear it "would violate HER civil rights"! The Minister for Labour & Social Affairs joined in on the attack, calling the practice of hijaab "savagery". What is amazing is that the school was run by Catholic nuns! Ask yourself this question: why is it okay for a nun to wear hijaab (because that's what it is) to please God, but a Muslim can't do it for the same reason? Isn't that hypocrisy? Or is it prejudice against Islaam?

This is perhaps the most insidious attack on the hijaab, when people claim it's for the good of our daughters. What they are saying is that we as Muslims are not fit to be parents and that they must step in to protect our daughters from us and from our beliefs! We see this arrogance surfacing everywhere.

When a girl comes to school in hijaab, her interrogation always begins with the same question: "Did someone tell you to wear this or did you decide for yourself?" Apparently we as parents are not allowed to guide our children towards Islaam; to do so is viewed as a form of child abuse. This has also happened in France with the following two sisters.

3. In France, Lila and Alma, two sisters aged 18 and 16, turned up to school in the hijaab. The school thought the parents must have "encouraged" the girls to wear the hijaab, however after investigating they

were shocked to discover that their father was an atheist Jew and their mother a non-practicing Algerian.

The father explained his daughters had come under no pressure from radical Muslims. "They have simply 'got God' – like so many teenagers always have – and their religion of reference happens to be Islaam," he said. The school was not happy and expelled both girls. They must now continue their studies from home.

When you hear of stories such as these, doesn't it make you think of oppression? What happened to freedom of choice? It's okay if a woman wants to wear less in this society, and it's okay for a man to dress like a woman; however, covering up for the sake of Allaah (Subhaanahu wa ta'aalaa) is seen as evil. You tell me: where is the logic in all that? This is oppression, when one can't be covered and practice his or her religion.

In the West everyone says we have freedom of religion, but do we really have it? If the West is acting this way, it makes me think that we haven't come very far in accepting people for who they are; we are still judging them on how they dress and we are treating them that way. So, next time you see a Muslim woman wearing the hijaab, remember that she is not oppressed; as a matter of fact, she is liberated, and her obedience to Allaah (Subhaanahu wa ta'aalaa) is more important to her than fashion and glamour.

"A head covering on a Muslim is a political statement but it is not when on a Christian nun's head."

Riem Spielhaus, Humbolt University

ACTION PLAN

1. If you're a woman try the hijaab for a day and see how it feels to be a Muslim woman. What tests did you go through wearing it for the day?

2. Next time you see a Muslim woman wearing hijaab, say, "Hi." This is a good deed, and also will make them feel that they are not being judged by everyone out there.

3. Most Muslim women wear the hijaab out of their conviction and longing to adhere to their faith and a sense of chastity. Spread this understanding amongst your family and friends.

Reflections on this chapter

_____

_____

_____

_____

_____

_____

_____

_____

_____

_____

_____

CHAPTER 6

Life Lessons From The Greatest Man

"What do you mean, you don't drink? Everyone drinks sometimes. I mean, we all need a beer to unwind," said Matt.

"To be honest with you, I have never drunk any type of alcoholic beverage in my life. The way I unwind is going home, taking a shower, and praying. Truly, this is when I am at peace," Abdullah replied.

"Pray? Are you kidding me? I haven't prayed in years. I went to the church on Sundays when I was a kid, but that was because my parents made me. Yeah, for me I need a cold beer and a burger and I am in heaven. What's the point of praying anyways? Everyone is always fighting with one another over what the true religion is. Isn't it just better to just be kind to everyone and not pray to any one God? I mean, we are all human beings, who cares which God we worship?" said Matt.

"Very good question, Matt. Let me ask you something. What if you invented a computer? You were the only inventor. You made it, and since you made it, only you knew how to work it. Would you leave a manual behind to help others use it? Or would you expect them to just play with it and figure it out?" Abdullah asked.

"I would leave a training manual explaining how to use it. Otherwise, they could break it doing whatever they want with it," Matt replied.

"Then how can God Almighty create us and not leave a manual on how to live our lives the way that will be best for us? He created us, and He knows what is good for us and what is not. He knows the things which will harm us and the things which will bring us benefit and peace. This is why God Almighty sent us messengers and books to follow," said Abdullah.

"That's interesting, I never thought of it that way. The issue is, how do we know who has the right book? The right way? Everyone claims it is theirs. How do you find out who is right and who is wrong?" Matt asked.

"This is the question that I asked myself when I began searching for the truth. One thing we must always remember is that truth stands on its own, whereas falsehood can't," said Abdullah.

"That's true, but how can you tell the difference when all of the books seem similar to each other?" asked Matt.

"Well, the first thing that I would do is go to a quiet place, alone; somewhere where no one can see you or talk to you or know that you're there. Be alone. Then, while you are there, talk to God Almighty. Ask Him alone, as the Creator of the worlds, to guide you to the right path: to the truth, to the religion that He has sent, which is perfect. You see, God sent down the Torah and the Gospel of Jesus (Peace Be Upon Him) as well as the Qur'aan; however, humans changed the Torah by hand as well as the Gospel of Jesus (Peace Be Upon Him). Did you know that the Qur'aan is the only book of God that hasn't been altered or changed since its inception? It's the same book that an African reads in Africa, while a Chinese reads it in China, a white person in America, or an Arab in Dubai. Anyone who wants to read the Qur'aan must learn some Arabic, no matter what background they have," said Abdullah.

"That's amazing. I don't think I have ever heard of people around the world praying the same exact way. I know that you can go to two churches that are similar but they may have different books they follow or teach. To be able to have only one book for all of the Muslims seems amazing. And the fact that no one alters and changes it is quite interesting," Matt replied.

At that moment, the phones began ringing. Abdullah and Matt both departed to their cubicles to get the rest of their work done for the day. Break was over.

....

"We never sent any Messengers before you who did not eat food and walk in the marketplace. But We have made some of you a trial for others to see if you will be steadfast. Your Lord sees everything."

(The Qur'aan: Chapter 25, Verse 20)

"The Prophet (Peace Be Upon Him) said: I guarantee a house in the surroundings of Paradise for a man who avoids quarrelling even if he were in the right, a house in the middle of Paradise for a man who avoids lying even if he were joking, and a house in the upper part of Paradise for a man who made his character good."

(Bukhari)

"My choice of Muhammad to lead the list of the world's most influential persons may surprise some readers and may be questioned by others, but he was the only man in history who was supremely successful on both the religious and secular levels."

Michael Hart (from The 100: A Ranking of the Most Influential Persons in History)

Thomas Carlyle said: *"They called him a prophet, you say? Why, he stood there face to face with them, here, not enshrined in any mystery, visibly clouting his own cloak, cobbling his own shoes, fighting, counseling, ordering in the midst of them. They must have seen what kind of a man he was, let him be called what ye like. No emperor with his tiaras was obeyed as this man in a cloak of his own clouting. During three and twenty years of rough, actual trial, I find something of a veritable hero necessary for that of itself."*

"There is no compulsion in religion."

(The Qur'aan: Chapter 2, Verse 256)

"Good and evil are not alike. Repel evil with what is better. Then he, between whom you and him there is enmity, will become as though he was a bosom friend."

(The Qur'aan: Chapter 41, Verse 34)

"Beware! Whoever is cruel and hard on a non-Muslim minority, or curtails their rights, or burdens them with more than they can bear, or takes anything from them against their free will; I (Prophet Muhammad) will complain against the person on the Day of Judgment."

(Abu Dawood)

Abdullaah ibn 'Amr said, *"The Prophet of Allaah, upon him be peace, was never obscene or coarse. Rather, he used to tell us that the best among us were those with the best manners."*

(Bukhari)

Al-Hasan ibn 'Ali ibn Abi Taalib (may Allaah be pleased with them both) said:

"I memorized from the Messenger of Allaah (peace and blessings of Allaah be upon him): 'Leave that which makes you doubt for that which does not make you doubt, for truthfulness is certainty and tranquility, whilst lying is doubt and confusion.'"

(Tirmidhi)

Anas bin Malik (RadiyAllaahu 'anhu'), who was raised in the Prophet's (Peace Be Upon Him) household and served him for many years, spoke of his matchless kindness:

"The Messenger of God (Peace Be Upon Him) would busy himself with the remembrance of God; he would not talk in vain. He would lengthen his prayers and shorten the speech, and he would not hesitate to help and take care of the needs of a needy, poor or widow."

(Ibn Hibbaan)

Abu Dharr said:

"I was walking with the Prophet (Peace Be Upon Him) in the Harrah (volcanic region) of Madeenah and we faced the Mount of Uhud; the Prophet (Peace Be Upon Him) said: 'O Abu Dharr!'
I said: 'Here I am, O Messenger of God!'
He said: 'It would not please me to have an amount of gold equal to the weight of Mount Uhud, until I spend and give it out (in the sake of God) within a night or within three nights. I would keep a single silver piece of it to help those who are in debt.'"

(Bukhari)

Three Solid Truths:

Once, a person was verbally abusing Abu Bakr (RadiyAllaahu 'anhu') while the Prophet (Peace Be Upon Him) was curiously watching with a smile. After taking much abuse quietly, Abu Bakr responded to a few of his [detractor's] comments. At this, the Prophet exhibited his disapproval, got up and left. Abu Bakr caught up with the Prophet and wondered, *"O Messenger of Allaah, he was abusing me and you remained sitting. When I responded to him, you disapproved and got up."*

The Messenger of Allaah responded,

"There was an angel with you [as you were] responding to him. When you responded to him, Shaytaan (Satan) took his place."

He then said,

"O Abu Bakr, there are three solid truths: If a person is wronged and he forbears it (without seeking revenge) just for the sake of Allaah (Subhaanahu wa ta'aalaa)*, Allaah will honor him and give him the upper hand with His help; if a person opens a door of giving gifts for cementing relationships with relatives, Allaah will give him abundance; and, if a person opens a door of seeking charity for himself to increase his wealth, Allaah will further reduce his wealth."*

(Mishkaat & Musnad Ahmad)

Once Prophet Muhammad (Peace Be Upon Him) was resting under a tree after returning from an expedition and hung his sword from the tree. A non-Muslim man came quietly, took hold of the sword, and addressing the Prophet, said to him:

"O Muhammad! Now who will save you from my hand?"

The Prophet heard it, rose up from his seat and said:
"Allaah will save me."
Hearing the name of Allaah, the man was overawed and the sword slipped from his hand. The Prophet rose up from his place, took the sword into his hand, and questioned him:
"Now who will save you from my hand?"
He felt sorry and begged him for forgiveness. The Prophet forgave him. He was so impressed by this kindness that he embraced Islaam. He then went to his tribesmen and expressed that he never found a man better than Muhammad (Peace Be Upon Him).

(Bukhari)

The Moderate Path:

A'ishah (RA) said:

*"The Prophet (Peace Be Upon Him) was not given a choice
between two matters, except that he would choose the
easier of the two, as long as it was not a sinful act. If that
act was a sinful act, he would be the farthest from it. By
God! He never avenged himself. He only became angry
when people transgressed the limits and boundaries of
God; in that case he avenged [for the sake of God]."*

(Bukhari)

As for his courage and bravery under normal circumstances
Anas ibn Malik said:

*"The Messenger of God (Peace Be Upon Him) was the best
of people and the most courageous. One night, the people
of Madeenah were frightened and headed towards the
sounds they heard during the night. The Messenger of God
(Peace Be Upon Him) met them while coming back from
the place of the sound, after he made sure that there was no
trouble. He was riding a horse that belonged to Abu Talhah
without any saddle, and he had his sword with him. He was
assuring the people, saying: 'Do not be frightened! Do not
be frightened!'"*

(Bukhari)

"Once, I was walking with the Messenger of God (Peace Be Upon Him) while he was wearing a Yemeni cloak with a collar with rough edges. A Bedouin grabbed him strongly. I looked at the side of his neck and saw that the edge of the cloak left a mark on his neck. The Bedouin said, 'O Muhammad! Give me [some] of the wealth of God that you have.' The Messenger of God (Peace Be Upon Him) turned to the Bedouin, laughed and ordered that he be given [some money].'"

(Bukhari)

Another example of his patience is the story of the Jewish Rabbi, Zaid bin Sanah. Zaid had given something as a loan to the Messenger of God (Peace Be Upon Him). He himself said:

"Two or three days prior to the return of the debt, the Messenger of God (Peace Be Upon Him) was attending the funeral of a man from the Ansaar. Abu Bakr and Umar, Uthmaan and some other Companions were with the Prophet (Peace Be Upon Him). After he prayed the funeral prayer he sat down close to a wall, and I came towards him, grabbed him by the edges of his cloak, and looked at him in a harsh way, and said: 'O Muhammad! Will you not pay me back my loan? I have not known the family of Abdul-Muttalib to delay in repaying debts!'

"I looked at Umar ibn al-Khattaab; his eyes were swollen with anger! He looked at me and said: 'O Enemy of God, do you talk to the Messenger of God and behave towards him in this manner? By the One who sent him with the truth, had it not been for the fear of not entering the Heavenly Gardens, I would have beheaded you with my sword!'

"The Prophet (Peace Be Upon Him) was looking at Umar in a calm and peaceful manner, and he said: 'O Umar, you should have given us sincere counseling, rather than to do what you did! O Umar, go and repay Zaid his loan, and give him twenty Sa'a (measurement of weight) extra because you scared him!'"

Zaid said: *"Umar went with me, and repaid me the debt, and gave me over it twenty Sa'a of dates. I asked him: 'What is this?'*

"He said: 'The Messenger of God (Peace Be Upon Him) ordered me to give it, because I frightened you.'"

I then asked Umar: 'O Umar, do you know who I am?'

Umar said: 'No, I don't. Who are you?'

Zaid said: 'I am Zaid ibn Sanah.'

Umar inquired: 'The Rabbi?'

Zaid answered: 'Yes, the Rabbi.'

Umar then asked him: 'What made you say what you said to the Prophet (Peace Be Upon Him) and do what you did to him?'

Zaid answered: 'O Umar, I have seen all the signs of prophet-hood in the face of the Messenger of God (Peace Be Upon Him) except two – (the first) his patience and perseverance precede his anger and the second, the harsher you are towards him, the kinder and more patient he becomes, and I am now satisfied. O Umar, I hold you as a witness that I testify and am satisfied that there is no true god worthy of being worshipped except God alone, and my religion is Islaam and Muhammad (Peace Be Upon Him) is my Prophet. I also hold you as a witness that half of my wealth, and I am among the wealthiest people in Madeenah. I give for the sake of God to the Muslims.'

Umar said: 'You will not be able to distribute your wealth to all the Muslims, so say, 'I will distribute it to some of the followers of Muhammad (Peace Be Upon Him).'

Zaid said: 'I said, then I will distribute (the apportioned) wealth to some of the Muslims.'

Both Zaid and Umar returned to the Messenger of God (Peace Be Upon Him). Zaid said to him: 'I bear witness that there is no true god worthy of being worshipped except Allaah alone, and that Muhammad (Peace Be Upon Him) is the slave of God and His Messenger.' He believed in him, and witnessed many battles and then died in the Battle of Tabook while he was encountering the enemy - may God have mercy on Zaid.'"

(Ibn Hibbaan)

"Whoever seeks refuge with God against your evil, then do not harm him. Whoever asks you by God, then give him. Whoever invites you, then accept his invitation. Whoever does a favor for you or an act of kindness, then repay him in a similar manner; but if you do not find that which you can reward him with, then supplicate God for him continuously, until you think you have repaid him."

(Ahmad)

Narrated 'Abdullah bin 'Amr:

"A man asked the Prophet, 'What sort of deeds or (what qualities of) Islaam are good?'
The Prophet replied, 'To feed (the the people) and greet those whom you know and those whom you do not know.'"

(Bukhari)

Abu Sufyaan Ibn Harb: Hercules' Impression

Al-Bukhari, on the authority of Ibn Abbaas, narrated that, "Hercules sent for Abu Sufyaan and his companions, who happened to be trading in Ash-Sham, Jerusalem. That was during the truce that had been concluded between the polytheists of Quraysh and the Messenger of Allaah, peace be upon him. Hercules, seated amongst his chiefs of staff, asked, 'Who amongst you is the nearest relative to the man who claims to be a Prophet?'

I (Abu Sufyaan) replied: 'I am the nearest relative to him from amongst the group.' So they made me sit in front of him and made my companions sit behind me.

Then he called upon his translator and said (to him), 'Tell them (i.e. Abu Sufyaan's companions) that I am going to ask him (i.e. Abu Sufyaan) regarding that man who claims to be a Prophet. So if he tells a lie, they should contradict him (instantly).'

'By Allaah, had I not been afraid that my companions would consider me a liar, I would have told lies,' Abu Sufyaan later said.

Abu Sufyaan's testimony went as follows: 'Muhammad descends from a noble family. No one of his family happened to assume kingship. His followers are those deemed weak with numbers ever growing. He neither tells lies nor betrays others, we fight him and he fights us but with alternate victory. He bids people to worship Allaah alone with no associate and abandon our fathers' beliefs. He orders us to observe prayer, honesty, and abstinence and maintain strong family ties.'

Hercules, on hearing this testimony, turned to his translator, bidding him to communicate to us his following impression, which reveals full conviction in the truthfulness of Muhammad's Prophethood: 'I fully realize that Prophets come from noble families; he does not affect any previous example of prophethood. Since none of his ancestors was a monarch, we cannot then allege that he is a man trying to reclaim his father's monarchy. So long as he does not tell lies to people, he is for the more reason immune to telling lies as regards Allaah.

'Concerning his followers being those deemed weak with numbers ever growing, it is something that goes in agreement with questions of faith until the latter assumes its full dimensions geographically and demographically. I have understood that no instance of apostasy has as yet appeared among his followers and this points to the bliss of faith that finds its abode in the human heart. Betrayal, as I see, is alien to him because real Prophets hold betrayal in abhorrence.

'Bidding worship of Allaah with no associates, observance of prayer, honesty and abstinence and prohibition of paganism are traits bound to subject to him all my possessions. I have already known that a Prophet must arise but it has never occurred to me that he will be an Arab from among you. If I was sure I would be faithful to him, I might hope to meet him, and if I were with him, I would wash his feet.' Hercules then requested that the Prophet's letter be read.

The observations of the emperor and finally the definite and clear-cut exposition of the Islamic message could not but create a tense atmosphere amongst the clergy present at the court. We were ordered to go out."

Abu Sufyaan said, 'While coming out, I said to my companions, "The matter of Ibn Abi Kabshah (i.e. Muhammad, Peace Be Upon Him) has become so prominent that even the King of Banu Al-Asfar (i.e. the Romans) is afraid of him." So I continued to believe that Allaah's Messenger (Peace Be Upon Him) would be victorious, till Allaah made me embrace Islaam.'

The king did not embrace Islaam, for it was differently ordained. However, the Muslim envoy was returned to Madinah with the felicitations of the emperor."

From: *The Sealed Nectar: Memoirs of the Noble Prophet (Peace Be Upon Him)*
I will share some *ahadeeth* (plural of hadeeth) with you that show Islaam supports tolerance and gentleness instead of violence and terror:

"Beware of the plea of the oppressed, for he asks Allaah Most High only for his due, and Allaah does not keep one who has a right from receiving what is due."

(Bayhaqi)

"The strong man is not the good wrestler; the strong man is only the one who controls himself when he is angry."

(Bukhari, Muslim)

"Do not be a people without a will of your own, saying that if others treat you well, you will also treat them well and if they do wrong, you will do wrong; but accustom yourselves to do good if people do good and do not do wrong if they do evil."

(Tirmidhi)

"If anyone walks with an oppressor to strengthen, knowing that he is an oppressor, he has gone forth from Islaam."

(Bayhaqi)

Alphonse de Lamartaine (a poet, member of the provisional government, and one-time presidential candidate) said in *Historie de al Turquie*:

> Never has a man set for himself, voluntarily or involuntarily, a more sublime aim, since this aim was superhuman; to subvert superstitions which had

been imposed between man and his Creator, to render God unto man and man unto God; to restore the rational and sacred idea of divinity amidst the chaos of the material and disfigured gods of idolatry, then existing. Never has a man undertaken a work so far beyond human power with so feeble means, for he (Muhammad) had in the conception as well as in the execution of such a great design, no other instrument than himself and no other aid except a handful of men living in a corner of the desert. Finally, never has a man accomplished such a huge and lasting revolution in the world, because in less than two centuries after its appearance, Islam, in faith and in arms, reigned over the whole of Arabia, and conquered, in God's name, Persia, Khorasan, Transoxiana, Western India, Syria, Egypt, Abyssinia, all the known continent of Northern Africa, numerous islands of the Mediterranean Sea, Spain, and part of Gaul. 'If greatness of purpose, smallness of means, and astonishing results are the three criteria of a human genius, who could dare compare any great man in history with Muhammad? The most famous men created arms, laws, and empires only. They founded, if anything at all, no more than material powers which often crumbled away before their eyes. This man moved not only armies, legislations, empires, peoples, dynasties, but millions of men in one-third of the then inhabited world; and more than that, he moved the altars, the gods, the religions, the ideas, the beliefs and the souls.' On the basis of a Book, every letter which has become law, he created a spiritual nationality which blends together peoples of every tongue and race. He has left the indelible characteristic of this Muslim nationality, the hatred of false gods and the passion for the One and Immaterial God. This avenging patriotism against the profanation of Heaven formed the virtue of the followers of Muhammad; the conquest of one-third of the earth to his dogma was his miracle; or rather it was not the miracle of man but that of reason. 'The idea of the unity of God, proclaimed amidst the exhaustion of the fabulous theologies, was in itself such a miracle that upon it's utterance from his lips it destroyed all the ancient temples of idols and set on fire one-third of the world. His life, his meditations, his heroic reveling against the superstitions of his country, and his boldness in defying the furies of idolatry, his firmness in enduring them for fifteen years in Mecca, his acceptance of the role of public scorn and almost of being a victim of his fellow countrymen: all these and finally, his flight, his incessant preaching, his wars against odds, his faith in his success and his superhuman security in misfortune, his forbearance in victory, his ambition, which was entirely devoted to one idea and in no manner striving for an empire; his endless prayers, his mystic conversations with God, his death and his triumph after death; all these attest not to an imposture but to a firm conviction which gave him the power to restore a dogma.

This dogma was twofold, the unity of God and the immateriality of God: the former telling what God is, the latter telling what God is not; the one overthrowing false gods with the sword, the other starting an idea with words.

Philosopher, Orator, Apostle, Legislator, Conqueror of Ideas, Restorer of Rational beliefs…

The founder of twenty terrestrial empires and of one spiritual empire, that is Muhammad. As regards all standards by which human greatness may be measured, we may well ask, is there any man greater than he?'"

ACTION PLAN

1. Read the Biography of the Prophet Muhammad (Peace and Blessings Be Upon Him).

2. Listen to lectures about him via CDs, or YouTube from the correct sources. I have some sources listed at the end of this book.

Reflections on this chapter

_____

_____

_____

_____

_____

_____

_____

_____

_____

_____

_____

_____

_____

CHAPTER 7

We Are All Human

"Want to mess with us? We will show you! This is America and you can't just come to our country and think you will rule with your Sharia! You hear me?" shouted the man in black clothes with a black ski mask in between kicks.

That one seemed to be the leader of the pack. He was the only one really talking. The other three men were just kicking and punching the 55-year-old man, who had been walking home from the mosque after Isha prayer.

"My religion doesn't teach us to kill innocent people. My religion teaches peace," the words were fumbled out of Ahmad's mouth.

"Peace? Peace? That's why you guys go around killing innocent people? They say that God tells them to do that in the Qur'aan. Your religion is not of peace. Your religion is of HATE! You guys need to get hurt too so that your people stop doing it to us!" yelled the man in the ski mask.

Blood started coming out of Ahmad's mouth. He was feeling terrible and was in pain. He couldn't move. All he could think about was his sick wife at home. She had cancer and could barely take care of herself. Would this put more stress on her and bring more stress to her?

He whispered to himself, "Yaa Allaah, please don't bring any more pain to my wife. Please make my kids help take care of her if I die. Yaa Allaah, please forgive me for my sins. I bear witness there is no God but You. I bear witness that Muhammad (Peace Be Upon Him) is the final messenger," Ahmad said as he lay on the sidewalk, bruised and bleeding.

He didn't know if he was going to live or die. He didn't know if anyone would call for help or just walk by him.

"Sir, are you okay? Sir, I have called for help, please hang in. Please hang in and keep breathing," Edmond said.

Edmond was just driving home from his security shift when he saw Ahmad lying on the concrete by the road. He knew immediately that this man was hurt. This was a nice neighborhood and there weren't any homeless people around.

As Edmond waited for the ambulance and police to arrive, he thought to himself, *Why would someone do this to someone else? I mean, if you want his wallet, take it, but why beat him up so badly, so much so that he looks like he's almost dead? What's happened to society? Why do people not care about other people anymore? Aren't we all human?* As he was thinking, tears rolled down his face. He quickly wiped them away, as he didn't want anyone to see him crying.

This could have been me. This could have been me. Would anyone have cared to stop and call 911? he asked himself.

The next thing Ahmad knew, he was in the hospital, and nurses were trying to check his blood pressure, temperature, and vitals.

"Ahmad, can you remember anything? We need all of the details to look for the guys who did this to you. Please try to remember. Can you tell me how tall they were? What ethnicity do you think they were? Were they white, black, Asian, Hispanic? Were they thin or heavy? Did they have an accent? Did you see the car they drove off in? Anything in particular that they may have done to stick out?" asked the police officer who was investigating the crime.

Ahmad kept going in and out of consciousness as the questions were being asked. He had no energy to answer them. Finally, after some time, the nurses called the detective as he was waking up again.

"Sir, my name is Robert and I am with the police department. Do you know where you are?" Robert asked.

Ahmad looked around. "I am in the hospital, I believe. Has anyone called my family?"

"Yes, they are in the waiting room. After I have talked to you, they will come in. Can you please answer my questions as well as you can, sir?" Robert asked.

Ahmad nodded his head.

As Robert left his hospital room, he was saddened to see another hate crime in his city. *What is wrong with people to just attack or kill people because of their faith? This is*

America; our First Amendment right is freedom of religion. Why can't we all get along? As he was thinking all of this, someone interrupted to tell him that some new evidence had been found with regards to another case.

Two weeks later, Ahmad received a call.

"Hi, sir, this is Robert with NYPD. How are you feeling? How is the family? I'm sorry, sir, we have tried our best and the new evidence we found was a dead end. We are not giving up, but I just wanted to give you an update. Please be safe and I will call you if anything comes up," said Robert as he hung up the phone.

....

Narrated by 'Aisha, the Prophet (Peace Be Upon Him) said,

"The most hated person in the sight of Allaah is the most quarrelsome person."

(Bukhari)

"It's easier to be ignorant and say I don't know about the problem. But once you know, once you've seen it in their eyes, then you have a responsibility to do something. There is strength in numbers, and if we all work together as a team, we can be unstoppable."

Craig Kielburger

"A person who has sympathy for mankind in the lump, faith in its future progress, and desire to serve the great cause of this progress, should be called not a humanist but a humanitarian, and his creed may be designated as humanitarianism."

Irving Babbitt

I decided to make a list of what all people have in common, and I wanted to share it with you. For once, I want you to forget race, religion, gender, and age. Look at this list and mull it over to understand what we all have in common:

1. We were all created by God the Greatest – Allaah (Subhaanahu wa ta'aalaa).

2. None of us chose which family or religion we were going to be born into.

3. None of us chose what our gender would be.

4. None of us chose how much we would weigh at birth.

5. None of us chose what our date of birth would be.

6. None of us chose the color of eyes, hair, and skin we would have.

7. None of us chose the situations that we would be born into.

8. All of us breathe.

9. All of us have fear.

10. All of us love.

11. All of us get angry.

12. All of us get sad.

13. All of us have basic human rights.

14. All of us have the right to live a life without oppression and torture.

15. All of us have a right to health treatment.

16. All of us have a right to be educated.

17. All of us have a right to eat.

18. All of us have a right to a fair trial.

19. All of us have a right to live in peace.

20. All of us will die someday.

The list could go on! As humanitarians, let's put aside our different beliefs, and just work on giving basic human rights to everyone all over the world. Basic human rights should not be limited because of race, religion, gender, or age. Basic human rights are owed to all of us; it doesn't matter what part of the world we are in, what ethnicity we are, which political party we follow, or what religion we practice. For once, let's think of everyone as a person, with the same needs that we have, and treat them with the same respect. Put aside your political views or worldly gains, and let's start treating humans like humans, and I say this message to myself first, and then to all of you. Let's unite for Basic Human Rights!

I would like to leave you with a few powerful quotes:

The Prophet, Muhammad (Peace Be Upon Him) said,

"Love for humanity what you love for YOURSELF."

(Bukhari)

"Help your brother, whether he is an oppressor or he is an oppressed one."

People asked, "O Allaah's Apostle! It is understandable to help him if he is oppressed, but how should we help him if he is an oppressor?"

The Prophet said, "By preventing him from oppressing others."

(Bukhari)

The greatest man (Peace Be Upon Him) explained us how to be with mankind in his final sermon.

"All mankind is from Adam and Eve, an Arab has no superiority over a non-Arab nor does a non-Arab have any superiority over an Arab; also a white does not have superiority over black nor a black have any superiority over white except by piety and good action. Learn that every Muslim is a brother to every Muslim and that the Muslims constitute one brotherhood. Nothing shall be legitimate to a Muslim which belongs to a fellow Muslim unless it was given freely and willingly. Do not, therefore, do injustice to yourselves.

Remember, one day you will appear before ALLAH and answer your deeds. So beware, do not stray from the path of righteousness after I am gone."

ACTION PLAN

1. When you look at Mankind, do so through glasses that are not tainted.

2. Educate yourself to understand all people as a whole by understanding their cultures and ways of life and try not to show any racism or generalization.

<u>Reflections on this chapter</u>

_____

_____

_____

_____

_____

_____

_____

_____

_____

_____

_____

RESOURCES

The Qur'aan: htttps://quran.com/

Frequently Asked Questions about Islam:
http://www.sultan.org/articles/ISLAMFAQ.html

Discovering Islam
http://discover.islamway.net/

The Purpose of Life (What does Islam say about it?)
https://www.islamtomorrow.com/purpose.htm

Purpose of Life – Audio Lecture
https://archive.org/details/ThePurposeOfLife-FullLecture-KhalidYasin

A Convert's Story: *Why I Chose Islam*
http://www.sultan.org/books/why_I_Chose_Islam.pdf

Embracing Islam
http://islamicweb.com/begin/converts_faq.htm

Islam and Science
http://www.islamicity.com/science/?AspxAutoDetectCookieSupport=1

Jesus in the Quran
http://www3.sympatico.ca/shabir.ally/new_page_24.htm

What did Jesus Really Say? (an amazing account of Jesus according to Islam)
https://islamhouse.com/en/books/193556/

This is Muhammad (SallAllaahu alayhe wa sallam)
http://mohammad.islamway.net/
Click on the language preference.

WEBSITES with interactive audio and beneficial lectures

The Deen Show, an interactive show for non-Muslims and Muslims alike
http://www.thedeenshow.com/

Peace TV: 24-hour Islamic International TV channel
http://www.peacetv.tv/

The Ideal Professional Speaker for Your Next Event!

"

Your presentation was interesting, informative, educational, fun, thought provoking, and one that students as well as members of the general public really enjoyed. I received many positive comments from those in attendance. They did not know what to expect but your presentation really opened their eyes to a culture they know little about and hopefully this experience will help them in future discussions with others. For many there, this was all new information for them as many students have never been exposed to the information in your presentation. Thanks for being so easy to work with and so wonderful with my students!

"

**Boyd Jones
Campus Programs Director
Winthrop University**

"

Zohra Sarwari has stood out as exceptionally creative and extraordinarily passionate about her topics. Her energy is contagious.

"

**Muhammad Alshareef
President, AlMaghrib Institute**

"

Zohra is one of the most relevant speakers I have ever heard. She takes a very serious topic and makes it easy to understand. The information Zohra provides is very timely and purposeful. I am sure your audience will appreciate her approach and effective delivery. Thanks for shedding some light on my world as well.

"

Stan Pearson II, MBA
Author - Speaker - Radio Personality

"

Zohra moved the audience with her dynamic, informative presentation, giving us all a perspective that serves to make us better people.

"

Diane Ingram, ACC Speaker,
Author, Coach

"

Zohra Sarwari is an exceptional campus speaker. She brought realism, compassion, and a bit of humor to a subject that many Americans know little about, aside from what they've been told by the mainstream media. We received nothing but positive feedback about Zohra's speech, from both students and community members. Thank you, Zohra, for sharing the gift of knowledge with our campus.

"

Faith Barnes
Student Activities, Owens Community College

Zohra Sarwari was very ENGAGING and successfully CAPTIVATED her audience. She was able to present visuals and demonstrated knowledge of her materials. At the end, she was encircled by students who wanted to talk to her and to purchase her books.

Catherine Rue
Student Life Administrator,
Northampton Community College

I highly endorse Zohra Sarwari's presentation "No, I'm Not a Terrorist", which Zohra presented on our campus in February of 2017. Zohra presented to a packed house with energy, integrity, and humility, as she connected with our students in a powerful way. At the conclusion of her talk, at least 30 students lined up to speak with her, and she patiently spoke with each student to answer their questions. Students told me how much they benefited from her talk, and how much they learned as a result of her presentation. Zohra is an incredible person to get to know. She's extremely flexible and easy to work with, her main goal is to promote understanding and acceptance, something we need more of in our world today.

Ron Buchholz, Director
University of Wisconsin-Whitewater
Career & Leadership Development – *"Helping Students
Achieve Their Dreams"

"I wanted to let you know the Zohra was absolutely incredible this evening! The crowd left very happy and learned so much. Thank you for working with us to bring Zohra to Clarion! It was such a pleasure working with you. I'm very happy we were able to have this presentation! Thanks so much!"

Sarah Zerfoss
Clarion University of Pennsylvania, PA

"I think that Zohra Sarwari did a phenomenal job during her lecture at UAB. The audience was very engaged, and her lecture was very informative and enlightening. Zohra was great to work with and engaging during conversation. Her pleasant demeanor was an added bonus. Overall, it was an awesome experience!!"

Jessica C. Nathan, M.Ed. |Coordinator of Student Activities
Office of Student Involvement & Leadership
UAB | The University of Alabama at Birmingham

We invited Zohra Sarwari to be the featured speaker at our Annual Sisterhood Dinner. Five minutes after we filled out her online interest form, we received a call from Zohra. She is one of the most humble, sweetest, and funniest people you'll ever meet. After a few minutes going over the program, she was eager to custom make a speech to match what we were looking for. On the day of she and her family arrived, she brought her own equipment and delivered an amazing speech. If you are looking for a great speaker, malleable to your budget, guaranteed to leave on impression on your audience – I highly recommend Zohra Sarwari without any hesitation. P.S. Make sure you take notes during her speech!

Jason Khurdan
Graduate Coordinator for Student Development
Rutgers University, Newark

Diversity Training Programs!

My name is Zohra Sarwari. I am a Muslim Woman who wants to work with your organization to achieve amazing results. My Diversity Training Programs are ideal for: law enforcement, TSA, hospitals, healthcare, corporations, universities, teachers, and high schools. I can help you empower your employees and team members with religious sensitivity training on Islam and Muslims.

WHAT SETS ME APART?

I share transformational knowledge, insight, and skills that help businesses experience true revitalization and growth. Each of my presentations covers areas from understanding the basics about the Muslim faith to workplace compliance policies and modern values that govern our faith. My speaking engagement at your firm can be tailored to your organization's schedule. We can work together to create that dream experience for your staff and other stakeholders in your business.

Based on the reviews and the feedback from my book, *No! I Am Not a Terrorist!*, and live lectures, I have seen thousands of people better understand the Muslim faith, and culture. My diversity training program is targeted to improve behavioral and social attitudes at your workplace.

HERE IS SOME HARD TRUTH:

Over the last decade, the issues surrounding diversity management and religious tolerance in the workplace have grown beyond a matter of compliance into an issue that determines a company's success. The reason is that there are deep-rooted cognitive biases which few people recognize that fuel their actions.

- Would you love to have an expert help you and your employees navigate the tides and create a more inclusive workplace experience?
- How about building stronger values such as religious tolerance?

It will also interest you to note that this can define your place as a responsible employer in the hearts of your staff. Within the workplace, individuals may choose to identify with a particular social group. People are born into different structured societies which make it normal for them to blend into different social categories e.g race groups, cultures, religions, and social groups. People tend to reflect these values on impulse but my training helps you set the right atmosphere in your organization.

LET'S MAKE IT HAPPEN

Just imagine having a group of people working together to create higher level of productivity irrespective of their religious differences – this is what I can make happen for you. You can contact me to speak at your next regional, seasonal meeting or conference.

Sincerely Yours,

Zohra Sarwari

For more information please email me at
Zohra@MuslimWomanSpeaker.com

Books By Zohra Sarwari

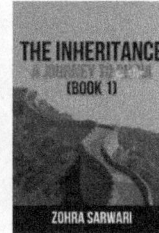

Have You Bought the Series "Things Every Kid Should Know: Drugs, Alcohol, Smoking, Bullying, Junk Food and Amr's Adventure in Europe" by Alya Nuri For Your Kids?

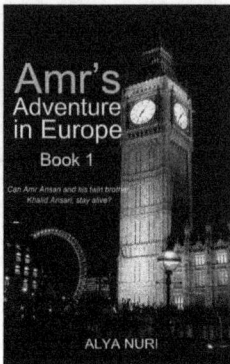

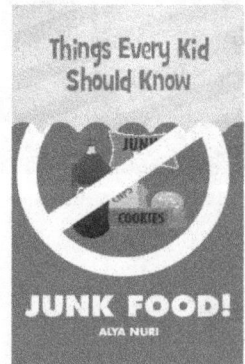

Have You Bought The Series "Things Every Kid Should Know: Strangers, Reduce, Reuse & Recycle, Fire **and Muslim Boys**" **by Zafar Nuri For Your Kids?**

Have You Bought The Series "Things Every Kid Should Know: **Hand Washing**", **Teeth and** Stealing" **by Arsalon Nuri For Your Kids?**

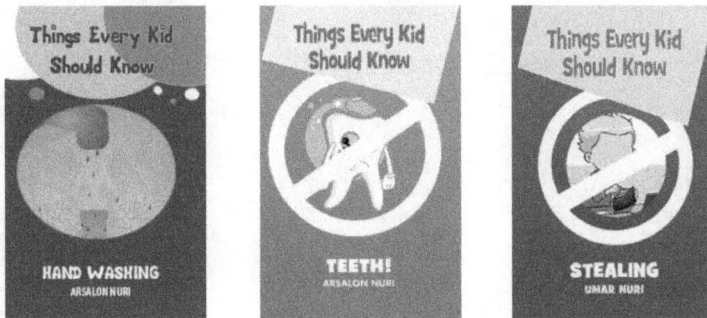

www.ingramcontent.com/pod-product-compliance
Lightning Source LLC
Chambersburg PA
CBHW031517040426
42445CB00009B/270